ANCIENT SECRETS OF THE WEALTHY

"In all thy getting get Understanding"

**Dedicated to my legacy and beautiful children
Nathaniel and Abigail**

Author WB Temm

Copyright 2013

Winston Bernard Temm 2013

All rights reserved. No part of this publication may be reproduced stored in a retrieval system or transmitted, in any form or by any means, electronic, mechanical, photocopying, recording, or otherwise, without written permission from the publisher or copyright holder.

TABLE OF CONTENTS

1. THE HABIT OF SAVING AND TITHING

2. MANAGE THE BACKDOOR

3. LEARN TO MULTIPLY

4. PROTECT YOUR INCOME

5. BECOME AN OWNER

6. BUILD A FUTURE INCOME

7. SEIZE THE OPPORTUNITY

8. BE A GIVER

9. BE CONSISTENT

INTRODUCTION

In **Deuteronomy 8:18**, God says, I have given you the power to get wealth, to establish my covenant. God wants to empower someone to walk in wealth and be a blessing to his or her generation, but are we willing to abide by the principles of His word. The ancient secrets of the wealthy is not a magic formula but principles that is condensed to open your eyes to the possibilities that anyone can overcome poverty and generate financial income to sustain him, his family and assist those in need. The ancient secrets of the wealthy are practical principles that must be executed, applied, and practiced for it to work in your life. You cannot read the information I'm about to share and not take action. Instead of writing a book containing unnecessary information, I have decided to write down the practical keys you can practice to attain wealth.

The book might just have a few pages to read but its content will alter the course of your life if applied. The secrets in this book were well tested and applied and have produced positive results. Many times it's the small foxes that spoil the vine. You and I most of the time has to make little adjustments to see our life move in the right direction. You might just need to make one or two adjustments to move forward and so it's my prayer that the simple truths in this book will bring you great joy and prosperity.

1st Secret: The Habit of Saving & Tithing

Matthew 25:23....*Well done, good and faithful servant! You have been faithful over a few things, I will make you ruler over many things*

"If you would be wealthy, think of saving as well as getting" **Benjamin Franklin**

Whenever it comes to the subject of money many church people become spiritual, yet they most of their prayers to God is for financial assistance. The reason why many people have holes in their wallets and banking accounts is because they don't save. Many people walk around assuming that money will come to them when they need it, but I believe money comes to those who know how money functions. Many people want cash flow to spend on a daily basis, but are ignorant of the fact that money must be channeled into an area of growth. When God created us he placed within us the ability to reproduce after its own kind. In Genesis 1, God blessed the first man saying; be fruitful and multiply. Every human being has been created by God to bring forth fruit, which refers to making money or receive some form of income.

The question we have to answer is are we people who save what we earn or do we spent every cent without thinking forward. It's very dangerous when your state of mind is not forward thinking. The habit of saving is a biblical principle that can be seen in the life of Joseph in the book of Genesis 37. Many of us are familiar with Joseph the dreamer and how he told his dreams to his brother of becoming a great leader and because of his dreams he was hated.

Joseph as we know was sold by his brothers to traders as a slave and then told the father that Joseph died. (Read Genesis 37 - 39) Joseph was then sold in Egypt unto a captain called Potiphar. Joseph went through temptation and false accusation in Egypt and landed up in the royal prison. This prison hosted men who offended the king of Egypt and was under the oversight of Joseph who was

placed as overseer over the prisoners.
The gift Joseph received from God was
to interpret dreams. The baker and
cupbearer were thrown in prison
because they offended the king. Both
of them had a dream and needed an
interpretation. Joseph being the
overseer of the prisoners had the
opportunity to interpret the dreams of
both the cupbearer and baker giving
them the exact time of its
fulfillment.

The king of Egypt received a dream and
no one in the whole kingdom could
interpret the dream and the cupbearer
who was restored back to his position
told the king of Joseph's gift to
interpret dreams. The purpose of why
Joseph was sold as a slave in Egypt
was now revealed. The king's dream was

a warning from God of a seven year famine that was going to take place and also of a seven year period of abundance. Joseph was given from God to Egypt to teach them the habit of saving. The king was instructed by Joseph how to develop a system of saving for seven years before the lean years approached.

The habit of saving in Egypt didn't just spare a nation but also the family of Joseph who came to Egypt to buy food when the famine was severe. The habit of saving is a lifestyle every individual has to develop until it becomes a state of mind. Savings is the lifestyle of those who understand the power of money and how it flows. Money attracts more money. Empty wallets don't attract money. God even compares money to himself because of the power money holds. Money does have power in itself only when it exchanges hands. The spirit, attitude, and desires of the person come upon the money he acquires. In other words money will magnify who and what we are when it's in our possession. Whenever you and I develop the habit of saving we harness the power that changes cities and nations; called money.

The saving that is required is simple yet requires discipline from your part. If you have ten coins, save one piece and use the nine. This has to be done on a consistent basis if you are to see growth in your finances. Many people don't practice the habit of saving and wonder why they are not entrusted with more. The bible is clear on this matter; he that is faithful in little SHALL be ruler over much. Your habit of saving and managing the little you have opens the door to increase and wealth in the near future.

Malachi 3:8 Will a man rob God? Yet you have robbed me. But you say in what have we robbed you? In the tithe and the offering!

Tithing is also ten percent of our monthly or weekly income we give to God to reveal our trust in Him. Tithing is also a sign of honouring God with our life, because money reflects our life. Through tithing God rebukes the devourer for your sake. You can save ten percent which is important; but tithing is God's way of blessing and making you fruitful.

Don't see tithing as a burden or something where the church demands money; look at it as a contract you have with the Creator of heaven and earth to be your source and provider. This means as long as you keep you part of the contract by tithing God is obligated to deal with bareness and the attack of satan against your finances.

Malachi 3:10 Bring all the tithe into the storehouse, so that there may be food in My house. And test Me now with this, says Jehovah of Hosts, to see if I will not open the windows of Heaven for you, and pour out a blessing for you, until *there is* not enough *room*.

Malachi 3:11 And I will rebuke your devourer, and he shall not decay the fruit of your ground against you; nor shall your vine miscarry against you in the field, says Jehovah of Hosts.

You cannot afford not to be part of this great promise; so make a decision today to involve God in your finances.

The enemies to saving and tithing are:

    1. Shorterm thinking
    2. Compulsive buying
    3. Mismanagement
    4. Undisciplined lifestyle
    5. Ignorance
    6. Disobedience

"When I was young I thought that money was the most important thing in life; now that I'm old I know it is"
Oscar Wilde

Here I have included another two practical tips on saving for young adults:

1. Learn self-control

If your parents are teaching you self control then you are fortunate but if not, then you have to learn the fine art of delaying gratification early to keep your finances in order. Although many can buy on credit it's advisable to save and purchase the item cash.

2. Take control of your financial future

If you don't learn to manage your income at an early stage; be aware there is someone out there that will mismanage your money for you. Whenever you begin to educate yourself then it will be impossible for some salesman, realtor, or con-artist to rob you of a bright financial future.

There is also another reason why many people don't save because they are intoxicated by name brands. I have no problem if you can afford the name brand but not at the expense of not paying your bond (House loan Repayment), car loan, children college fees etc. Too many individuals will enslave themselves to wear a certain name brand and when you ask them the total price of their three pair of shoes its equivalent to a deposit on a car. You may think I'm over exaggerating but our young adults have to learn that name brand doesn't give you a sense of identity or security. God doesn't supply all our name brands but all our current needs to fulfill his purpose and to live in peace.

Final word

If you spent every cent that you earn on a day to day basis without thinking of the future, then how will God be able to trust you with future wealth? You don't need many of the short-term luxuries you see; begin to develop a new state of mind, that says my future starts now.

2ND SECRET: MANAGE THE BACKDOOR

Luke 14:28 *For which of you, intending to build a tower, does not sit down first and count the cost, whether he may have enough to finish it;*

"If you know how to spend less than you get, you have the philosopher's stone" **Benjamin Franklin**

There is one thing that has been true for ages and that is, don't spend more than your earn. The problem with many individuals is not that there is a lack of money; the true lack is having no skill to manage the money entrusted to them. The scripture teaches us how to manage and count the cost before we

set out after anything. You may argue
the fact that how can you save and put
money away when what you earn is just
enough to support yourself and family.
The truth is that our earnings can
never gratify every desire which
usually reflects greed

You have to learn about delay
gratification. When you walk around in
the shopping mall and you can't
control your wants you will soon
demand your earnings to gratify
desires that are unnecessary. Closing
the back door is an important
principle because most of us are
burdened with desires that cannot all
be satisfied. Psychologists showed a
practical instance of delayed
gratification when they took a small
boy into a room and placed a

marshmallow on a plate in front of him . The lesson was if the child can wait for 15minutes he will get another marshmallow. The test shows that most children couldn't wait, some tried something to distract them but those who practiced delayed gratification was rewarded.

The scary part of this exercise was that most children who do not practice delayed gratification oftentimes have a personality growing up of not managing what they have but spend it all at once. An expert teaches that a child who wants to gratify every desire is harder to work with than a child who knows about delayed gratification. It's also a proven fact that those who can practice delayed gratification oftentimes become more successful later in their life. So the principle in this chapter is to remove all unnecessary wants and desires and write down only what is needed while developing a habit of saving. So if you save tenth percent of your income and use the ninety percent to cover the needed things you will be well on your way to building sustainable wealth.

The temptation you will face on a constant basis will be to spend your earnings on unnecessary wants. There is no greater deception into thinking that ungratified desires will cause you unhappiness. Someone who desires to drive an expensive car but still drive a small economical classic will be deceived into thinking not having the expensive car makes a person unhappy. The truth is both vehicles have only one purpose, driving you to a destination, desiring the expensive car is a burdened desire that many times cannot be gratified. The decision is then to look at what must be eliminated to close the backdoor of mismanagement and only concentrate on what is necessary.

Too many people never count the cost when they make debt and somehow think when they come to their senses the debt will disappear the next morning. The truth of the matter is you must sit down and calculate if you are willing to burden yourself and family because of wants and unnecessary desires or live a content lifestyle while building a sustainable bank balance, the choice is yours. So learn how to manage what you earn and have a financial plan how to cover expenses.

3RD SECRET: LEARN TO MULTIPLY

Genesis 1:28 *and God blessed them. And God said to them, be fruitful, and multiply and fill the earth, and subdue it*

You have to remember that when you begin to save up and your money growths as you learn to manage your finances; there will be the need to put that money to work. This means you have to learn ways and means to give your finances work to do so it can multiply and reproduce. God spoke to the first human beings in the beginning: Be fruitful and Multiply. The instruction was clear to mankind; learn to produce and grow. How many of us have in time past bought something expensive and the thing we bought couldn't multiply the money we spent to buy it with. This causes many people to stay stuck in life because they don't think about growing what they are saving and ends up spending what they have saved and repeat the same cycle all over again. If you look at the world of agriculture it works on a system of fruitfulness,reproducing and multiplying.

Can you imagine what would happen if there was no system of multiplying, being fruitful and reproduction? This principle is what we take for granted yet it's a God lesson to show mankind the secret to increase and building a sustainable future. Why not learn to employ your finances and allow it to labor for you and not vice versa. A rich man will tell you that the secret to staying wealthy is to create employment for your money to keep multiplying. As Christians God teaches us to give so we can create a window of opportunity where we will receive. The principle is not just to give money away but to employ your finances in the work of God or to do good so that you can create a window where men will give back to you.

The question in this chapter is simple, what can you do with your money to make it multiply. What can you buy in and sell again for your money to grow. What investment can you make to see what you have saved multiplies. Can you imagine using your finances to labor for you and allow it to grow and multiply? What will your savings look like in five or ten years from now? God will give you wisdom how to invest your money and cause it to grow if you will ask Him for wisdom. Whenever you take money as an investment tool to grow it without having an attitude of greed and stinginess your income will not just multiply but God will give you more ideas to build wealth and be a blessing to those in your sphere of influence.

Robert Kiyosaki said: *it's more important to grow your income than cut your expenses*

John Paul Getty said: Money is like manure. You have to spread it around or it will smell.

In plain and simple English today,
what can you do to employ your
finances to be your slave?

4TH SECRET: PROTECT YOUR INCOME

Matthew 6:21 For *where your treasure is, there will your heart be also.*

Protecting your savings will be as important as to growing your money. The purpose of guarding your finances is to make sure that you don't just lend to people because you have a good heart. The principle in this chapter is to make sure that whoever comes to ask or make some type of loan must and should have the ability to repay. You should also be very sensitive when people ask money for business ventures or starting a new project. This might sound nice to the ear or good on paper but until you have no track record of the person's skills or past ventures you will surely lose hard earned money. Too many of us allow our emotions to get the better of us when it comes to protecting our wealth. We pity people and the people we pity become the leeches that suck us dry.

Make sure today that you do some homework about investments before you invest your money. The bible says where your treasure is your heart will be also; which mainly speaks about having a good understanding and account of your finances. Some people have no record of income and expenditures. The greatest adjustment in your life will be protecting your money from loss. One of the schemes I can think of in the past was the pyramid scheme where many people never did their homework and made huge investments which caused great loss. You have to look at both sides of the coin when it comes to parting with your money.

Don't allow quick rich schemes rob you of your hard earned income. Do your own research and be sure if anything goes wrong that you have some sort of insurance to reclaim what was invested. Nothing is more devastating when you lose your money because your heart wasn't with your treasure. Don't take this advice for granted but be bold enough to protect what has been entrusted to you.

5TH SECRET: BECOME AN OWNER

Joshua 1:3 *Every place that the sole of your foot shall tread upon, I have given that to you..."*

The bible says that the earth is the Lord's and the fullness thereof. This should give you a sense of confidence knowing as a child of God you can have your own piece of property. The earth is God's personal property. When you begin to develop the habit of saving and growing your financial income it is also important that you try to move away from just renting a house to owning your own property. Many people today are more concern about what they wear, drive, and eat but yet having your own piece of ground should be more important than these things.

Matthew 6:25 Therefore *I say to you, Do not be anxious for your life, what you shall eat, or what you shall drink; nor for your body, what you shall put on.*

Owning your own house and property should be a goal you strive to achieve with the help of Almighty God. There should be the desire to put your family in their own house where you can plant your own garden and enjoy a lifelong investment. You may start out renting and be faithful to a landlord but don't let that be your ultimate goal;get your own property which is achievable. God will help you achieve that dream of having you own property if you are willing to practice some of these principles and put your faith to work.

Psalm 37:5 *Commit thy way unto the LORD; trust also in him; and he shall bring it to pass.*

Draw up your plan and goals and be clear about where you want to stay and commit it to the Lord to assist you in achieving your goal. I want to encourage you my friend, don't allow the economy to discourage you and place fear in your heart.

- God can do exceedingly abundantly above all you can ask or think.
- With God all things are possible.

- There is nothing to hard for the Lord.
- To them that believe all things are possible

My favorite scripture is whatsoever things you desire when you pray believe you receive it and you shall have it. (Mark 11) It's time to claim your inheritance and owning your own property is part of that inheritance. When God called Abraham in Genesis twelve God promised him land. When God spoke to Joshua He also promised him land. You are a child of God who is the Creator of the ends of the earth; claim your right to own land. Let this become part of your life's dream owning your own property and house.

6TH SECRET: BUILD A FUTURE INCOME

Proverbs 22:6 *Train up a child in the way he should go: and when he is old, he will not depart from it.*

It's a truthful fact that no one stays young forever. Our youth today seem to have a mindset that they will remain young forever and have their strength all their life. I must admit it took me a while to discover that you have to make some form of preparation for when you get old. Isn't it amazing that when you are in the prime of your life thinking of building a future is never part of life's journey? In fact many of our teenagers and young adults live for the moment not making any plans for the future. I personally think the reason for this is many are not informed about building a future income and so ignorance causes many to get old living in poverty.

The bible says train up a child in the way he should go; which makes it our responsibility as parents, teachers, leaders and religious leaders to train and inform the youth about building a future income. I have seen many old people who haven't been train in the way of building a future income and then depend on their children to take of them which should be a blessing but becomes more of a burden. Don't become a financial burden to others because you haven't made time to put away for the future. It has to become compulsory to this generation to be taught and trained to build a sustainable income for the future.

Make sure you take out life cover and draw up a will for yourself in the event if anything should happen to you that your family is provided for. The scary part many times is when there is only one bread winner in the house and there is no life insurance taken out to provide for the family in the event of death. This is something no one wants to think about yet we have a responsibility to build a future income to protect our family. Make it a priority even right now to get life insurance to build a sustainable income for the future. Don't leave your family or children in poverty because you neglect thinking of the future.

The bible says train up a child in the way he should go and when he is old..." God promises old age to the child that is trained in the way he should go. Doesn't this mean those who are responsible for educating, training and developing have the responsibility to fully prepare our youth?

Let us not allow ignorance and pride to overshadow the reality of building a future income.

7th Key: Seize the Opportunity

`Matthew 25:14-29

The story in Matthew 25 speaks of a man who went on a journey and left his property to three men entrusting each one with a certain amount of money and instructed them to increase it in his absence. The story reveals that two of the men took the advice and instructions and grew their income but the one who he gave the one talent buried his money and did nothing. When the master returned he called this man who did not use the opportunity to increase his income, lazy and wicked. All three had the opportunity to grow their finances but one of them didn't use the opportunity that was given to him. You will have numerous opportunities to increase and grow your income but will you seize the opportunity to do so ? What you do with opportunity will determine if you will see increase and success or suffer regret. There are two powerful twins that will work against your success and opportunities and they are procrastination and indecision. If you don't deal and remove these behaviours it will tie you to failure and stagnancy.

Opportunity comes to those who prepare and develop themselves. No one can seize the opportunity for you it's a personal desire and decision you have to make. Opportunity usually comes when you feel tired and frustrated. The moment opportunity comes it never reveals itself as opportunity but as a challenge. You can many times get a deal to do business, go to a meeting, buy goods at cheap prices and resell and all this will happen to you in the form of opportunity. There is a saying that goes, strike the iron while it's hot; this is so true when it comes to opportunity. The bible says today if you hear God's voice hardened not your heart; this refers to opportunity. If God gives instructions do not delay the opportunity to obey because your prosperity is linked to seizing the opportunity.

Benjamin Franklin said: You may delay, but time will not.

Johann Wolfgang van Goethe said:

"Every second is of infinite value"

Hazel Lee said: I held a moment in my hand, brilliant as a star, fragile as a flower, a tiny sliver of one hour. I dripped it carelessly, Ah! I didn't know I held opportunity.

Fight with all your might against delay, procrastination and indecisions for they are the demons of regret. There are certain moments and opportunities in life that can never be retrieved.Make sure that you don't allow fear to paralyze you when the opportunity presents itself. Fear is a spirit that's assigned to stop progression in your life. The bible says that God has not given us the spirit of fear but of love, power and a sound mind. You have to speak out against fear and know deep within your heart that if God is for you who can be against you. May you never back down when opportunity arises in fact when opportunity knocks you will have the boldness and wisdom to seize your God given opportunity.

8th Key: Be a Giver

Luke 6:38 *Give, and it shall be given unto you; good measure, pressed down, and shaken together, and running over, shall men give into your bosom. For with the same measure that ye mete withal it shall be measured to you again.*

Before we get to the last chapter I thought it would be proper to advise you on the importance of giving. Although the book is geared to encourage you to increase your income it would be ignorant of me not to include God's way of doing things. In fact giving is God's method to increase you and not decrease you. God's very nature is to give and when you want to live a prosperous life and experience open doors of favor and opportunities; learn a lifestyle of giving back to God. It's important that you find a local church that preaches and teaches the Word of God and commit yourself to giving. Do you know that the quickest way to sink your financial ship is to develop an attitude of selfishness and being stingy. The bible says it's more blessed to give than to receive. Doing good to the house of God and assisting people when it is in your power to do so will create open doors of opportunities.

2Corinthians9 says; he who sows or gives sparingly will also reap sparingly and He who sows or gives bountifully will also reap bountifully.

If you do good and it goes well with you why not lighten the burden of your fellow man. God expects us to give back to our churches, communities, and nation if we are blessed by Him.

Mother Teresa said: It's not how much we give but how much love we put into giving.

Proverbs 11:24 A man may give freely, and still his wealth will be increased; and another may keep back more than is right, but only comes to be in need.

Winston Churchill said: We make a living by what we get but we make a life but what we give.

I hope today you will realize that it is not always about accumulating and hoarding up for yourself but also to practice the principle of giving to increase exceedingly. Whatsoever you sow(give) you will reap is a principle that affects every human being so learn to sow(give) cheerfully so that God may call you bless and give you favor. This is a life principle that works anywhere in the world so take action today and be a blessing by giving.

9TH KEY: BE CONSISTENT

Anthony Robbins said: It's not what we do once in a while that shapes our lives. It's what we do consistently.

Jim Rohn said: "Success is neither magical nor mysterious. Success is the natural consequence of consistently applying basic fundamentals.

The only way you will see success in what you have read thus far is when you make a decision to take massive action and become consistent. The information you receive in such a compact way can further your life and increase your income or you can remain stagnant because you remain inconsistent.

The definition for the word consistent means: The state or quality of holding or sticking together and retaining shape. It also means a degree of firmness. The question is then pose to you are you willing to take action and be constant in practicing these principles until you see the required results? Or are you just ishing to be rich which is of little purpose.

Having general desires is a weak longing, but if you have a plan of action what you want and when you want it, God can bring that plan to pass. Stop living a life of just wishing and take the time to set out goals and a life plan and be consistent in working towards its fulfillment. Your improvement will happen if you develop an attitude of consistency. As I come to the conclusion of this book it's important that you realize your life will only change if you stop making excuses and make decisions that will move you forward.

Let's look at a biblical story in Luke 18

Luke 18:2 Saying, *There was in a city a judge, which feared not God, neither regarded man:*

Luke 18:3 And *there was a widow in that city; and she came unto him, saying, Avenge me of mine adversary.*

Luke 18:4 *and he would not for a while: but afterward he said within himself, though I fear not God, nor regard man;*

Luke 18:5 *Yet because this widow troubleth me, I will avenge her, lest by her continual coming she weary me.*

If you read this story you can clearly see how consistency was the key to this woman's breakthrough. You have to develop an attitude that says it's not over until God says you win. The problem with so many of us is we quit when we face any type of opposition. Develop a firmness in you that say I will never give up even when the answer and result doesn't seem to manifest. Yes you will face challenges, maybe fail or make bad decisions but stay consistent in reaching for your goals. Learn today that it's not your mistakes and failures that will define you but how well you rise after being knocked down. *I close with the words of Anthony Robbins: It's in the moment of our decisions that our destinies are shaped.*

More about the Author

WB Temm is residing in the beautiful City of cape Town South Africa. He is a husband, a father and a preacher of the Word of God. He is currently the overseer of three churches and travels extensively developing leaders and speaking prophetically to churches.

For more books of the Author please visit amazon.com /lulu.com or email wbtemmbooks@gmail.com

To stay connected to the author please follow him on these social networks.

Facebook page: Apostle Temm

Twitter: apostletemm

More Books

- God attraction
- Underdogs
- Shifting into your place of Enlargement
- The Language of Grasshoppers
- Taking off Limitations
- No longer Condemned
- Synchronize
- From the Cave to the Mountain
- Untie me
- What are you thinking?
- Finish your course

www.ingramcontent.com/pod-product-compliance
Lightning Source LLC
Chambersburg PA
CBHW071820170526
45167CB00003B/1379